Oklahoma State Capitol

Oklahoma City

Jane Moorman

There is a saying, "It was a Friday night and it seemed like a good idea at the time." That sums up the beginning of the State Capitols Project.

When I told my brother of my idea of photographing state capitols, he said, "You do know there are 50 states and two of them you can't drive to."

Each capitol has its own unique beauty that reflects the state's personality when it was built.

Jane Moorman, photographer

Cultural Diversity Apparent in the Capitol

The diverse cultures of the state are apparent throughout the capitol, from the state seal on the first floor to the artwork throughout the building.

The state seal includes the seals of the Civilized Tribes — Cherokee, Chickasaw, Choctaw, Creek and Seminole — as part of the symbolic design.

The capitol includes 18 rotating art exhibitions in the North, East and Governor's galleries. Each gallery features an element from the state flag, the symbols of which celebrate the high ideals and peace between its Native American and European settlers.

Architects Soloman Andrew Layton and S. Wemmyss-Smith designed Oklahoma's capitol in the Greco-Roman style in 1914.

The exterior is constructed mainly of Indiana limestone, complemented by a base of local Oklahoma pink and black granites. The interior prominently features marble throughout.

Original plans called for a dome, but it was omitted due to cost overruns in 1915. The money, labor and materials needed to fully complete the structure was diverted to the World War I effort.

As a temporary solution, a saucer dome was placed over the building's rotunda. Viewed from the interior of the building, it gave the appearance of a shallow dome.

In 2000, fundraising efforts to construct the new dome enabled the completion of the building in 2002.

The names of donors who contributed at least $1 million toward the $21 million construction are honored in the "Ring of Honor" at the base of the interior dome. Their names appear in six-inch gold letters, viewable from all points throughout the rotunda.

Flight of Spirit

Painter Mike Larson's *Flight of Spirit* is one of the many paintings in the capitol that honors the cultural influences in the state.

The painting features five world-renowned Native American ballerinas from Oklahoma. It merges the tragic history of Native Americans with the hope and renewal of modern accomplishments.

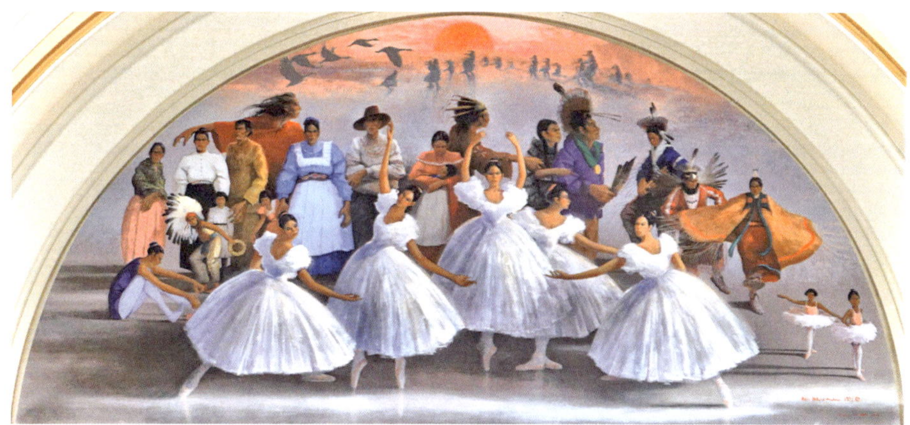

Behind the illuminated ballerinas is Larson's depiction of the Tail of Tears. Five geese soar over the displaced Native American, symbolizing the grace and spirit of the five ballerinas. Traditionally dressed Native Americans stand tall behind the ballerinas.

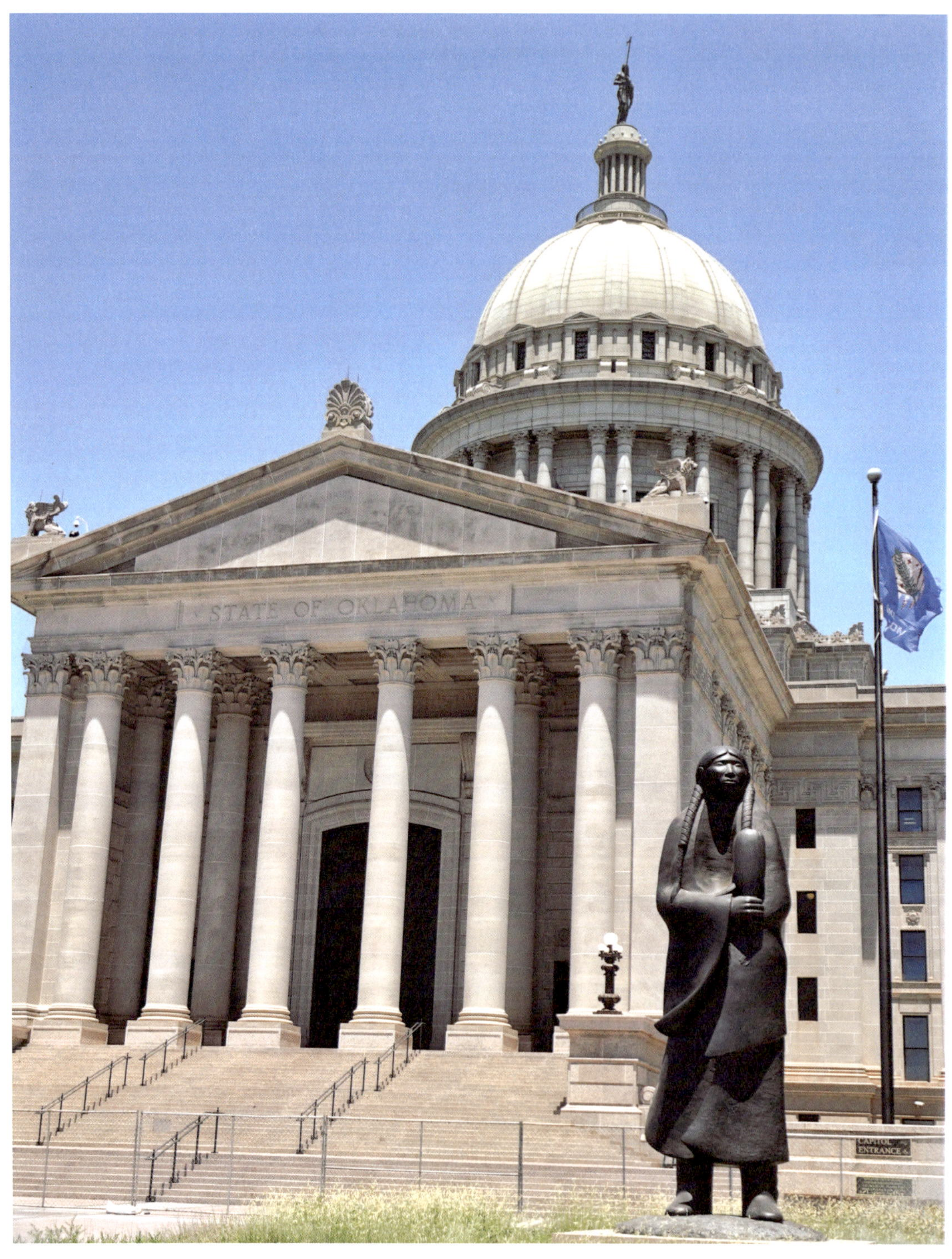

Dome Statue

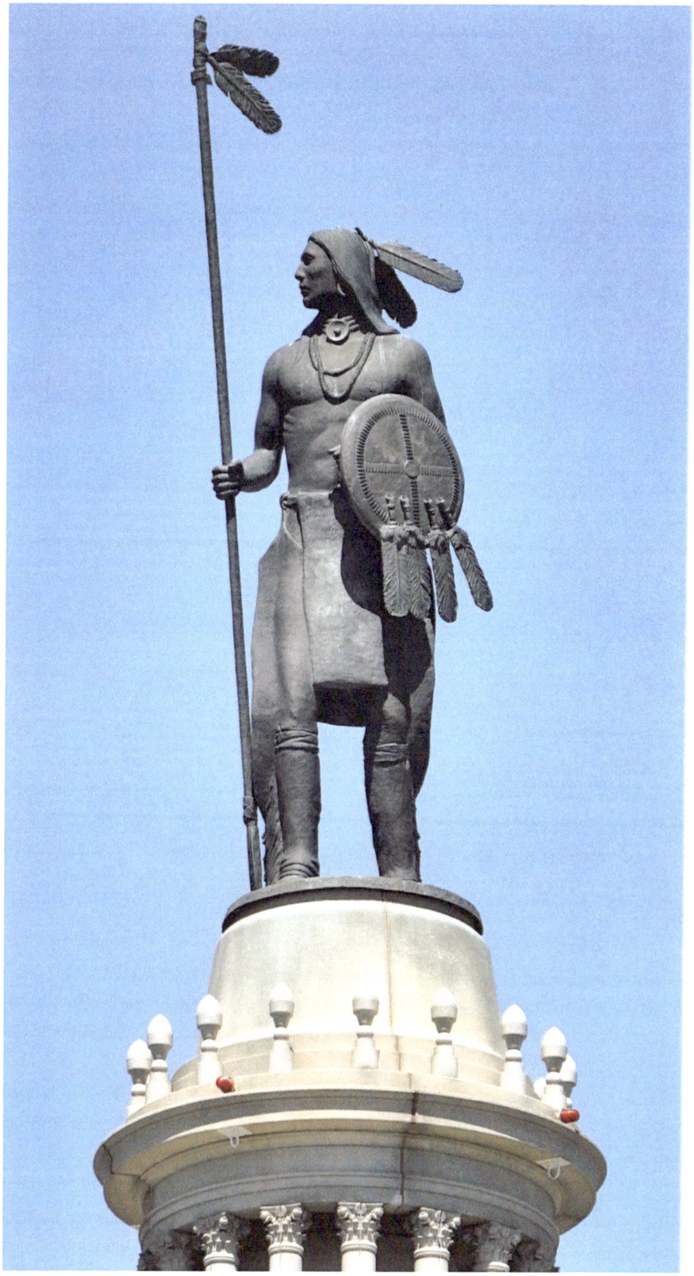

Oklahoma's capitol was without a dome from 1917, when the building's construction was completed, until 2002, when the dome was finally added.

A 17-foot statue named "The Guardian" tops the dome. Oklahoma Senator Kelly Haney, a Native American, sculpted the statue of a Native American warrior.

Although there was no dome or statue until 2002, a monumental tribute to Native Americans, "As Long as the Waters Flow," has stood guard on the capitol grounds since its dedication in 1989. (opposite page)

Allan C. Houser's 13-foot, 6-inch bronze reflects President Andrew Jackson's vow to Native Americans that they shall possess their land "as long as the grass grows, and the rivers run."

Lacking intricate detailing, the solid planes along the surface denote strength within an everlasting presence.

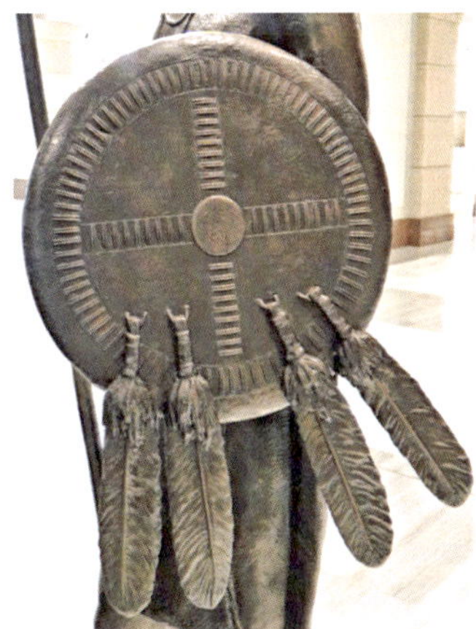
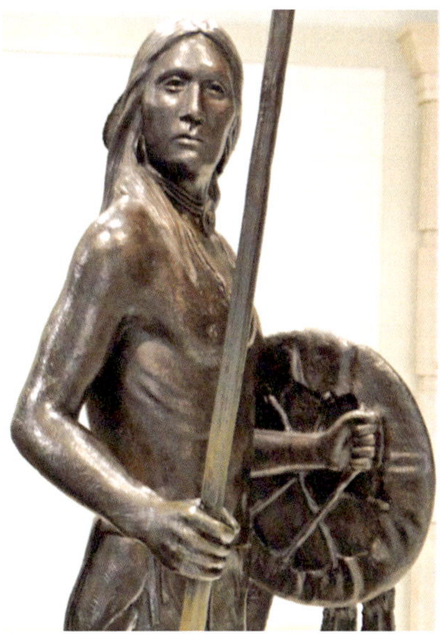

A replica of the dome statue is in the capitol's visitor entrance.

Main Entrance Bronze Doors

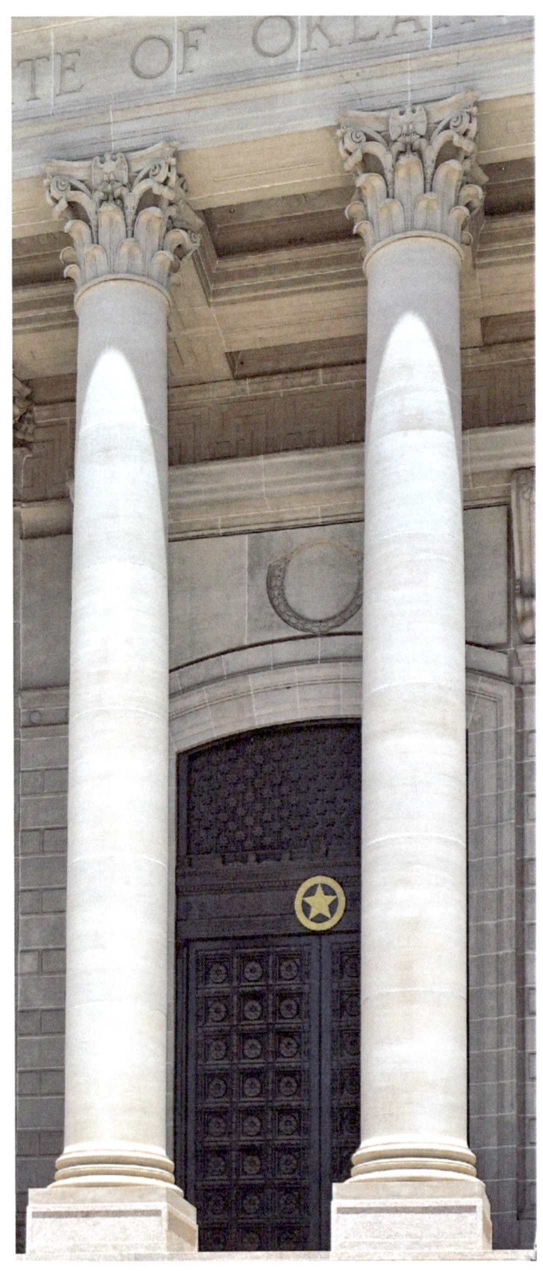

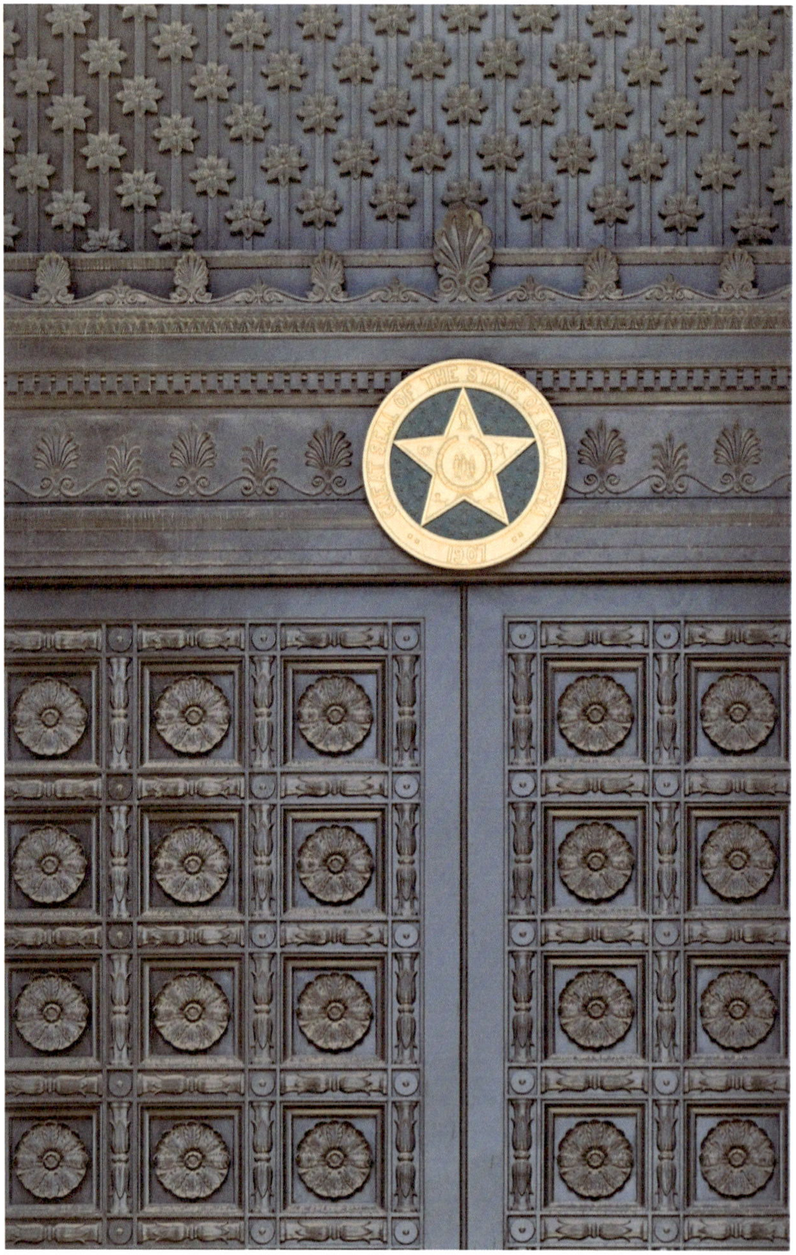

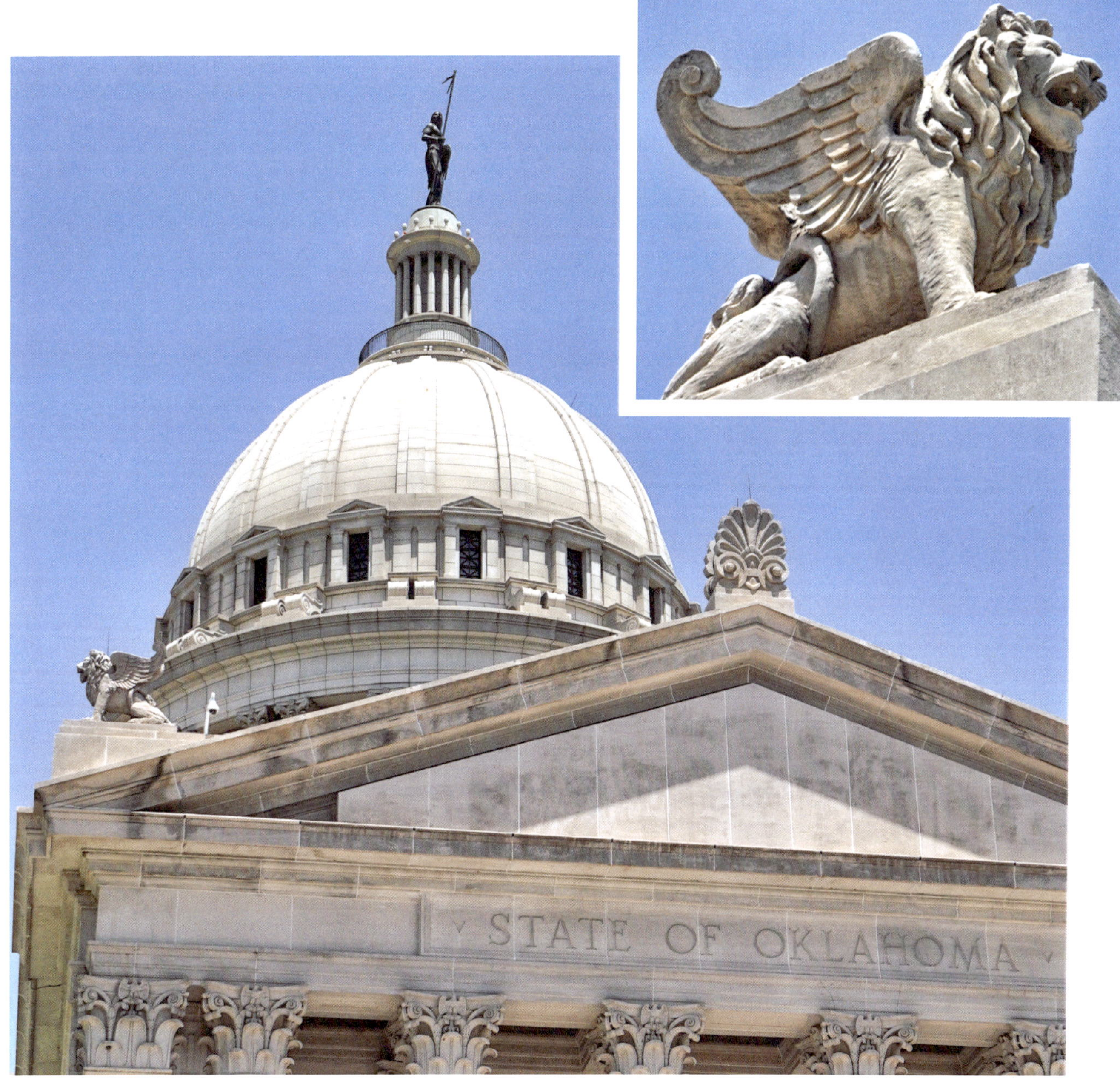

The State Guards the Memory of Her Dead

Pro Patria is a three-panel mural by Thomas Gilbert commemorating the tragedies and triumphs of World War I.

The artwork was dedicated on Armistice Day, Nov. 11, 1928. During the dedication, White declared, "Through these canvases, may the muffled voices from the grave speak to the generations to come of the day when men were not too proud to fight and held life less than their country's honor."

The central panel represents the courage an sacrifice of a brave soldier answering his country's call to war.

The right and left panels, titled *The State Guards the Memory of Her Dead,* honor fallen soldiers. White meticulously added the names of the 2,735 Oklahoma soldiers who died during World War I.

The side panels are viewed through the glass- walled conference rooms.

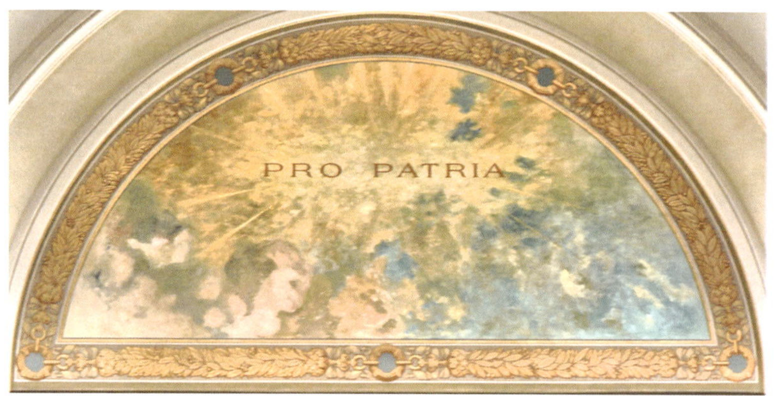

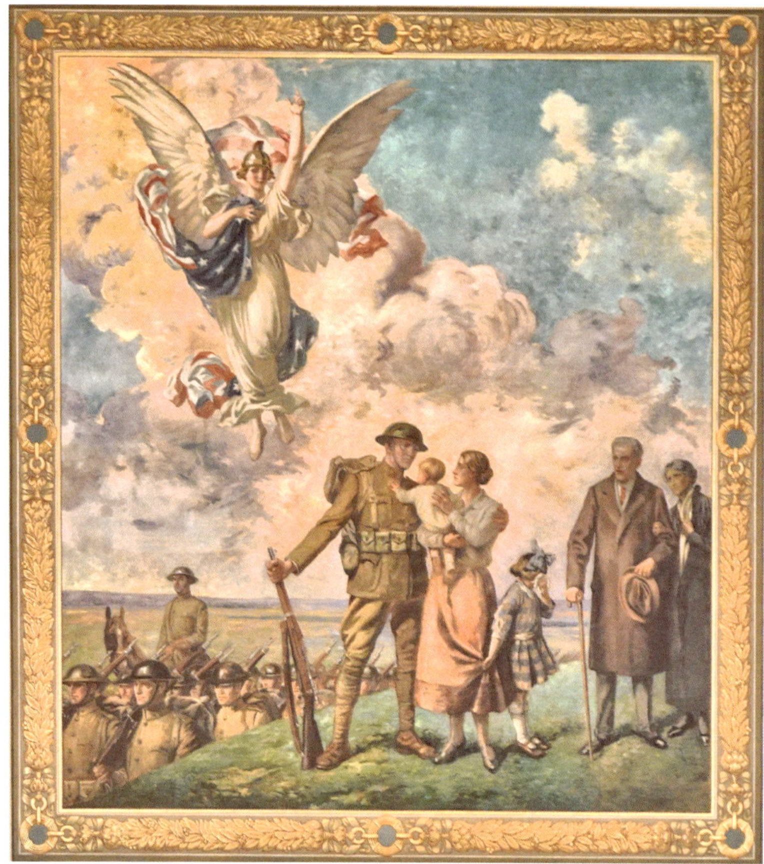

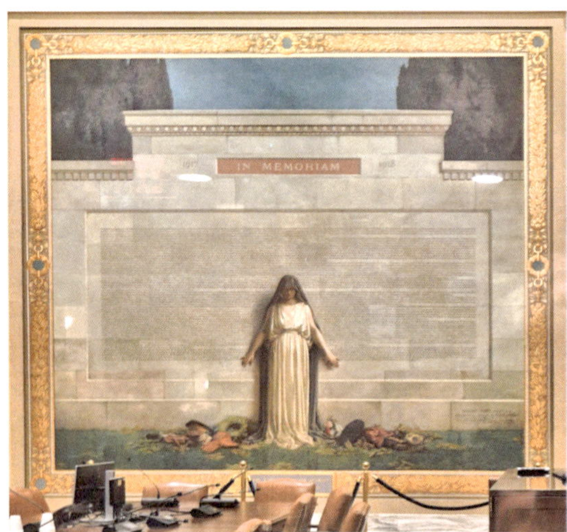

Grand Stairway: Stained-glass barrow ceiling

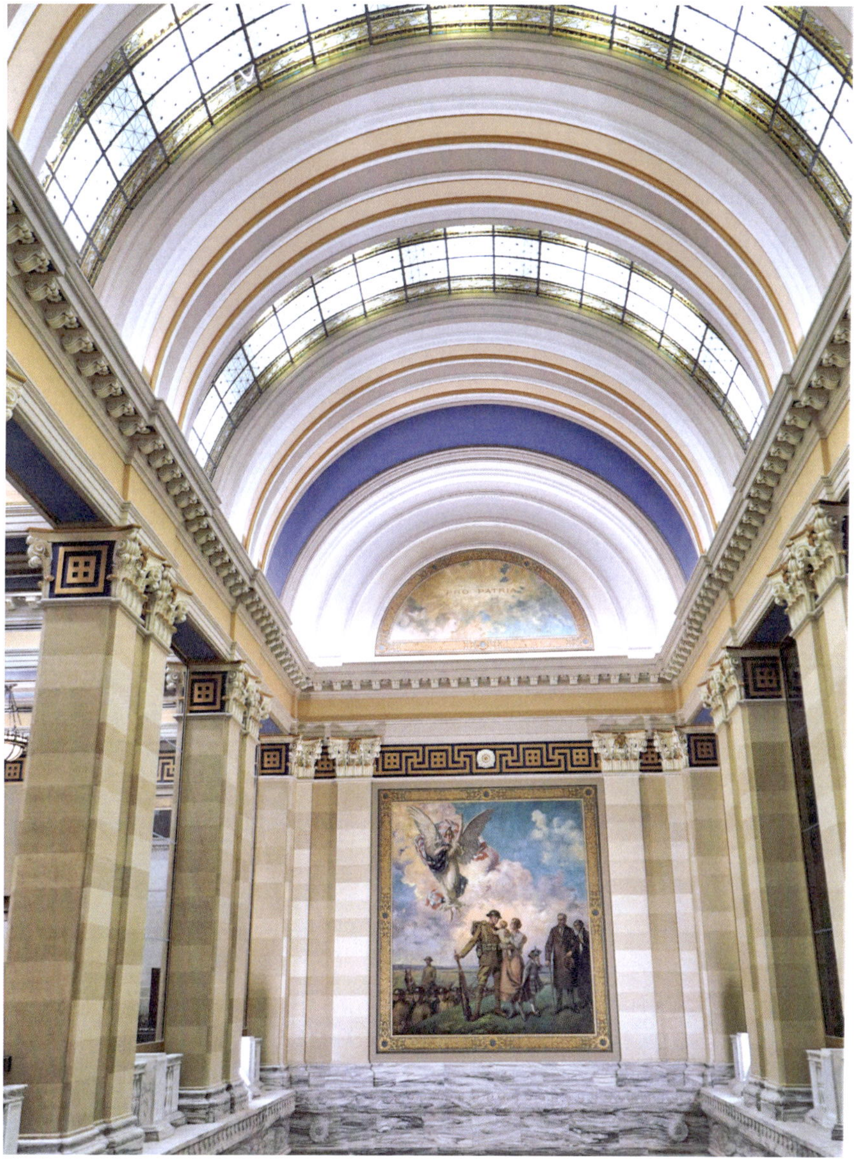

The Grand Stairway culminates at the fourth-floor rotunda where the Senate and House of Representatives chambers are located.

Flanking the stairway are conference rooms with special glass walls capable of providing privacy by becoming smoked glass.

Overhead is a stained-glass barrow ceiling with the Pro Patria artwork in the lunette.

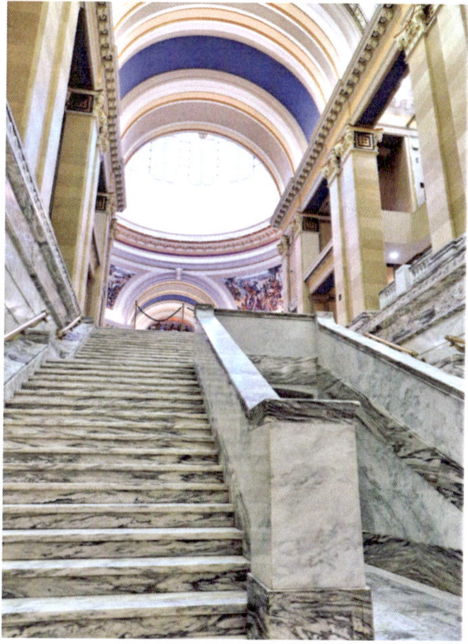

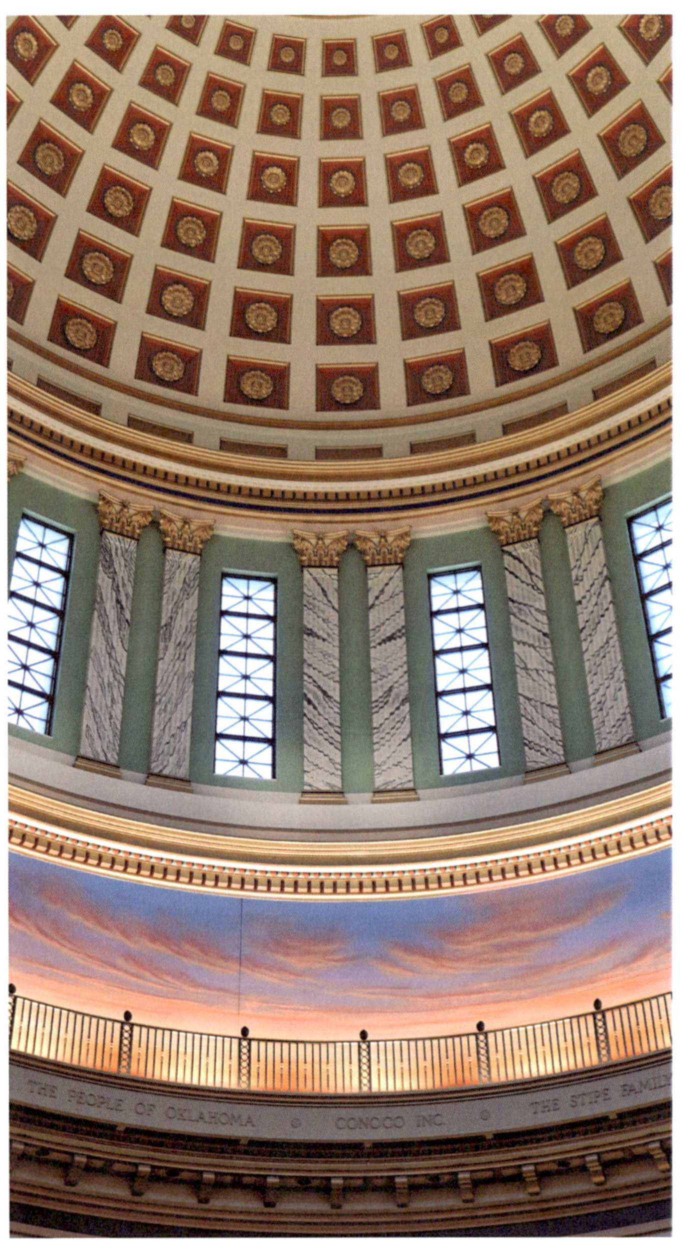
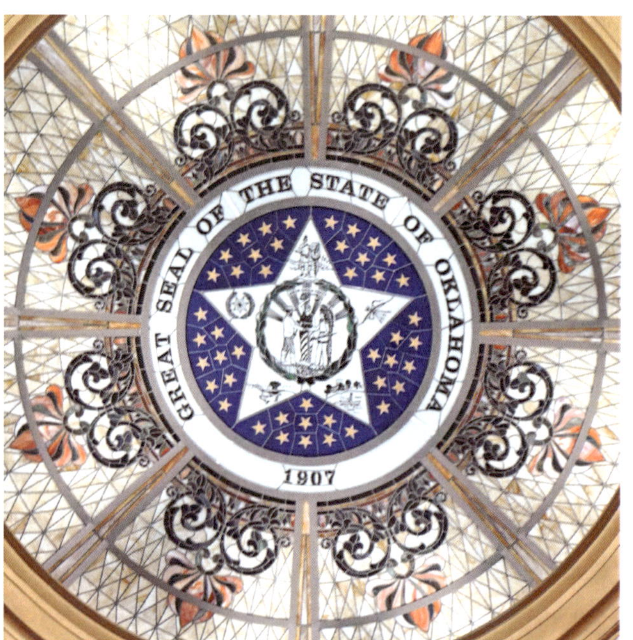
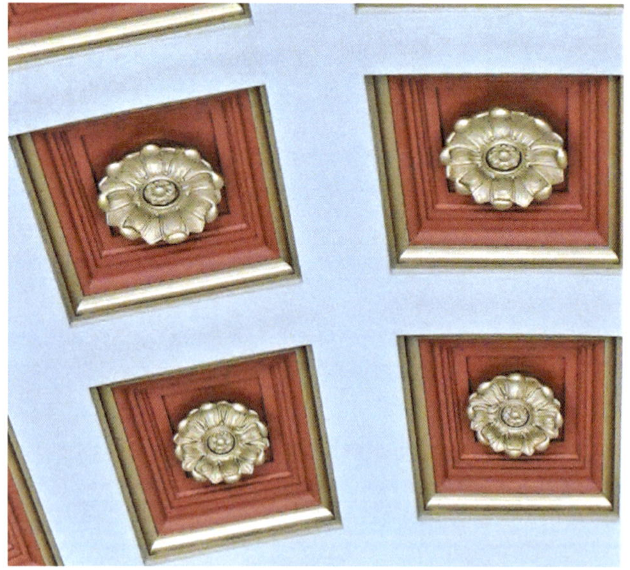

Rotunda Dome

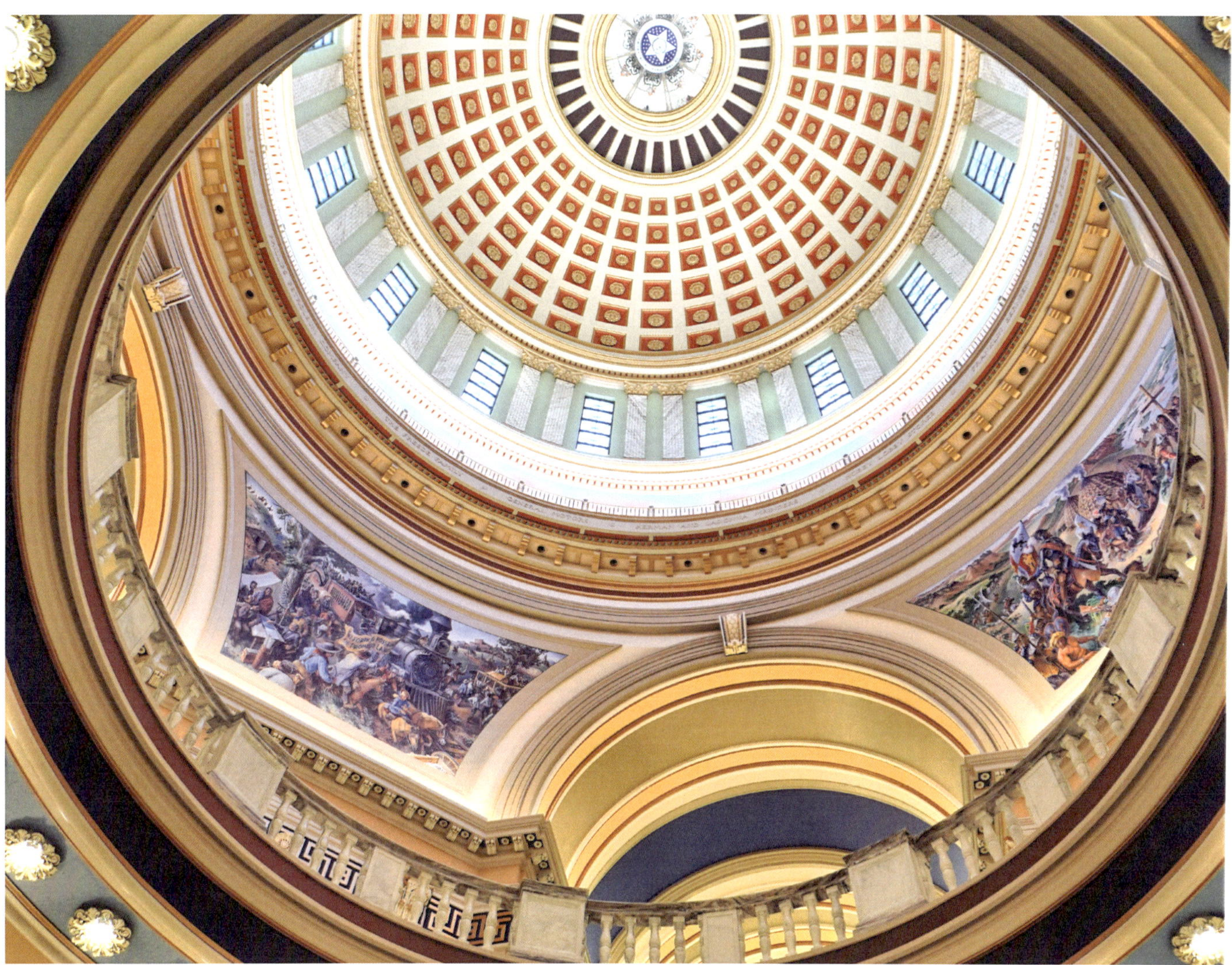

The crowning glory of the capitol's rotunda is the interior dome. The dome's color scheme symbolizes the state's rich Native American history and features bold red, orange, gold, and brown colors reminiscent of the state wildflower, commonly known as the Indian Blanket.

An original stained-glass interpretation of the Oklahoma State Seal graces the interior peak of the dome and features a color palette that harmonizes with the overall inner dome design.

Charles Banks Wilson Rotunda Murals

Charles Banks Wilson created the four 13-feet-by-27-feet murals depicting the history of Oklahoma.

The first mural, *Discovery and Exploration,* depicts famed Spanish explorer Franciso Vasquez de Coronado atop his armored horse.

In the mural *Frontier Trade,* Wilson depicts a bustling scene of rising commerce.

Indian Immigration captures the atmospheric tension and civil unrest as 67 different Native American tribes were forced into the region.

Non-Indian Settlement refers to when the unassigned lands were open to all in the Land Run of 1889.

Real people from that era are shown in the scenes.

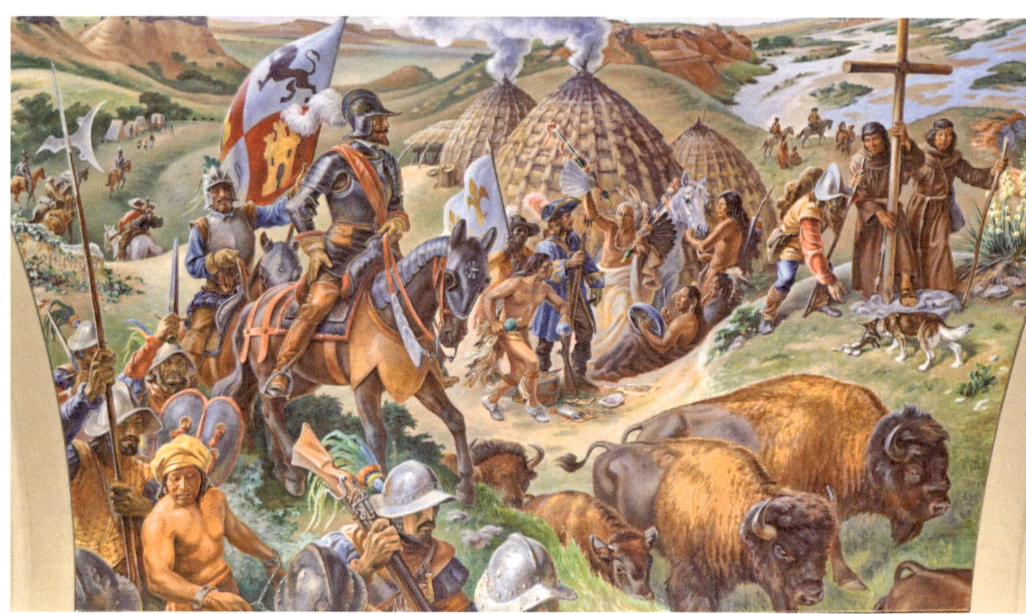

Discovery and Exploration 1541-1820

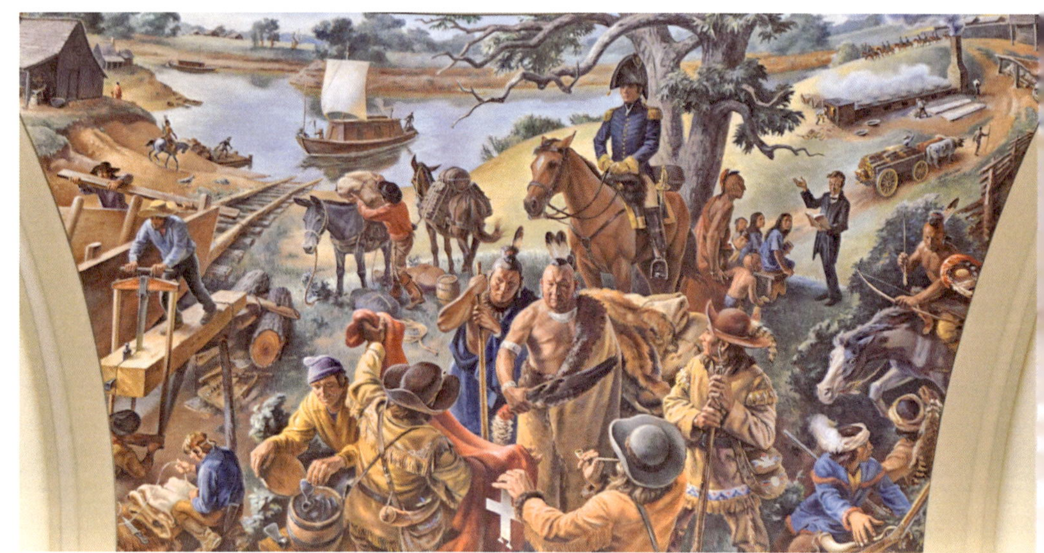

Frontier Trade 1790-1830

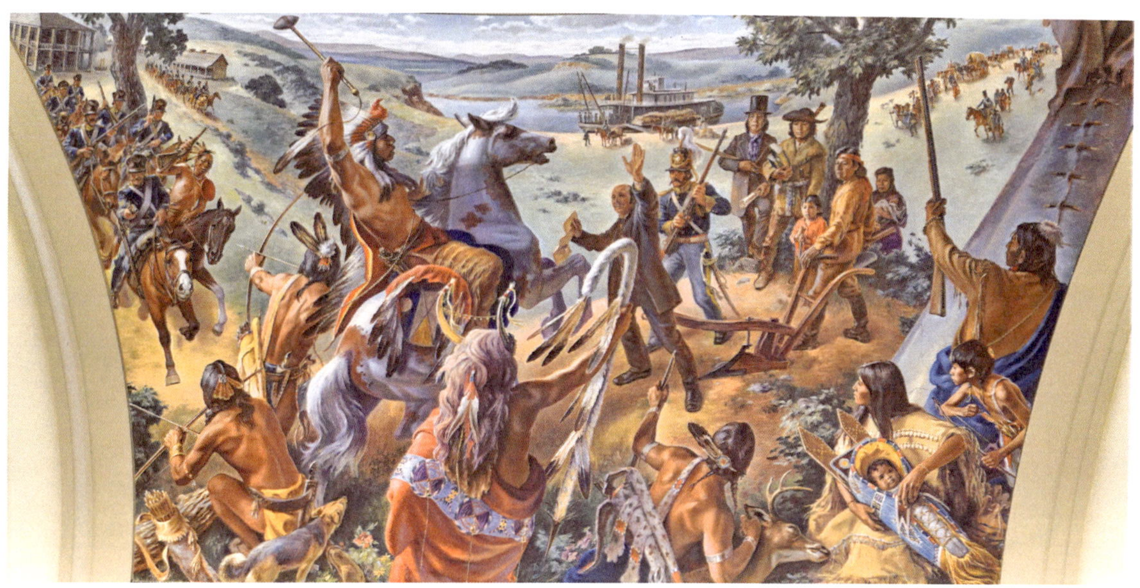

Indian Immigration 1826-1865

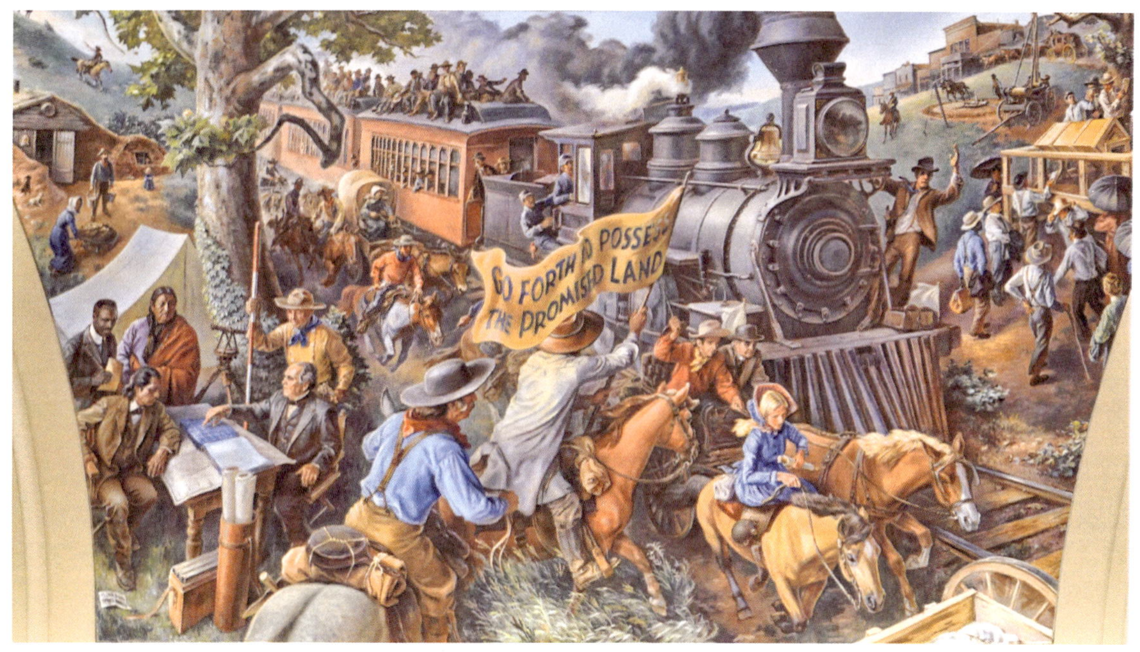

Non-Indian Settlement 1870-1906

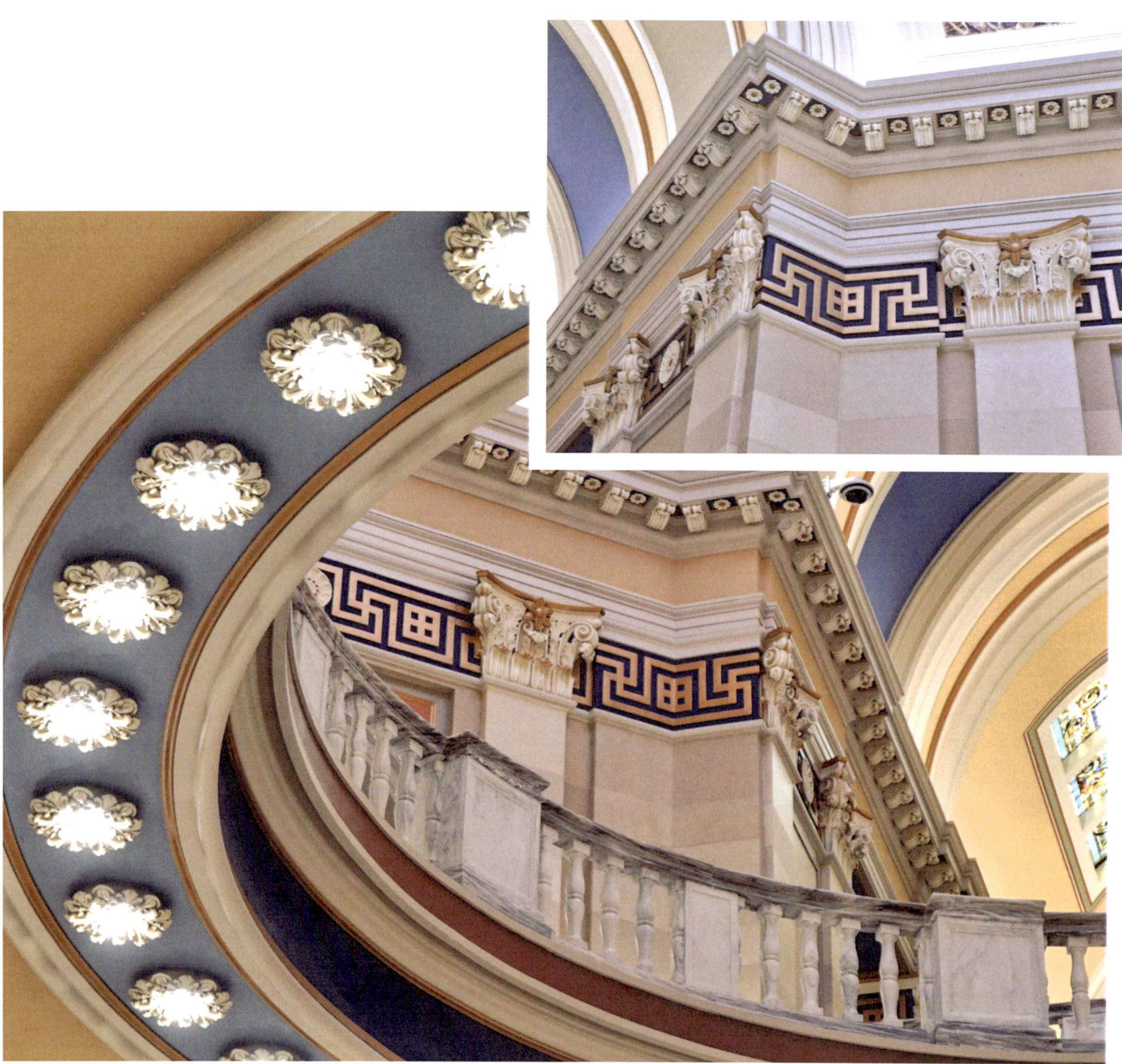

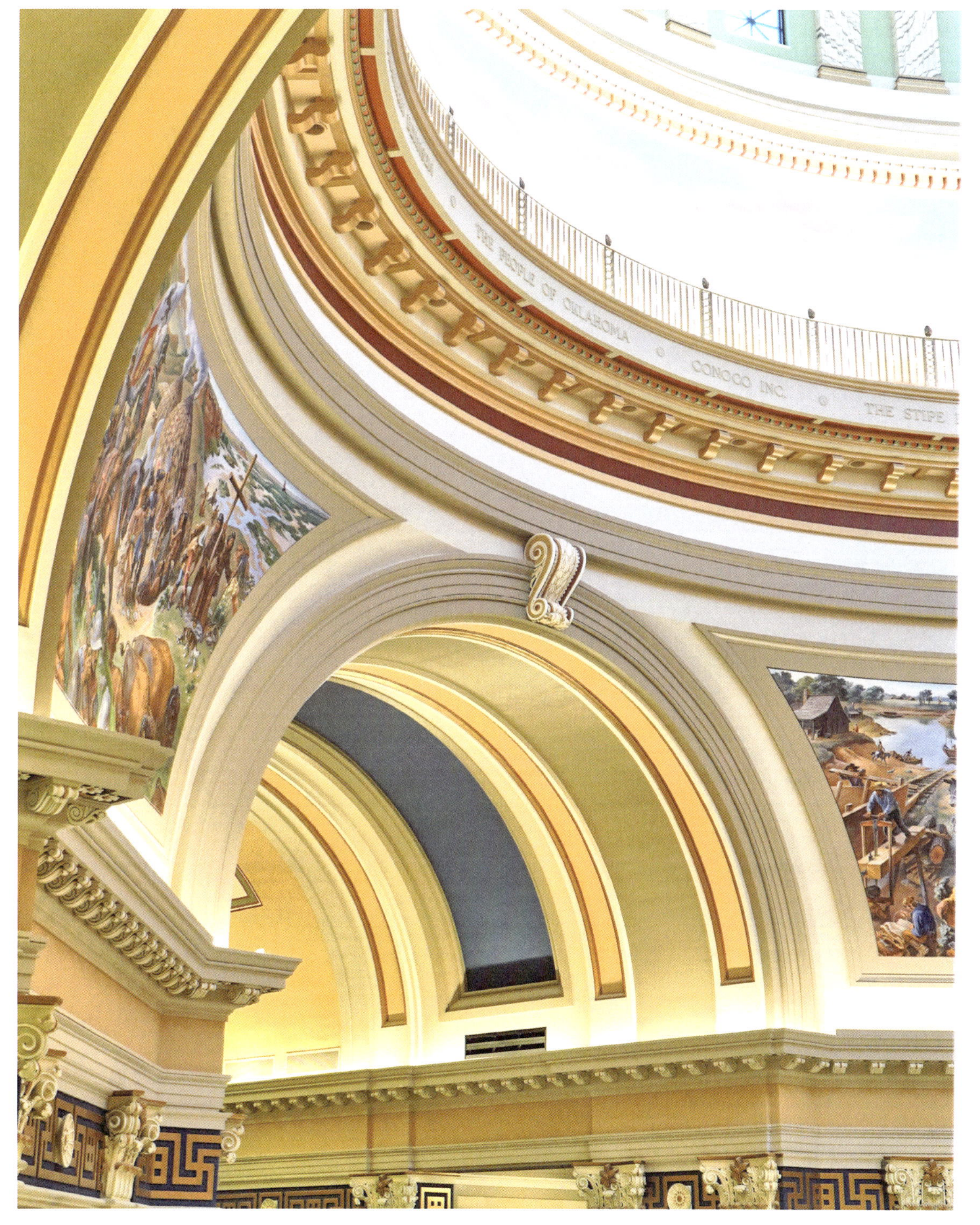

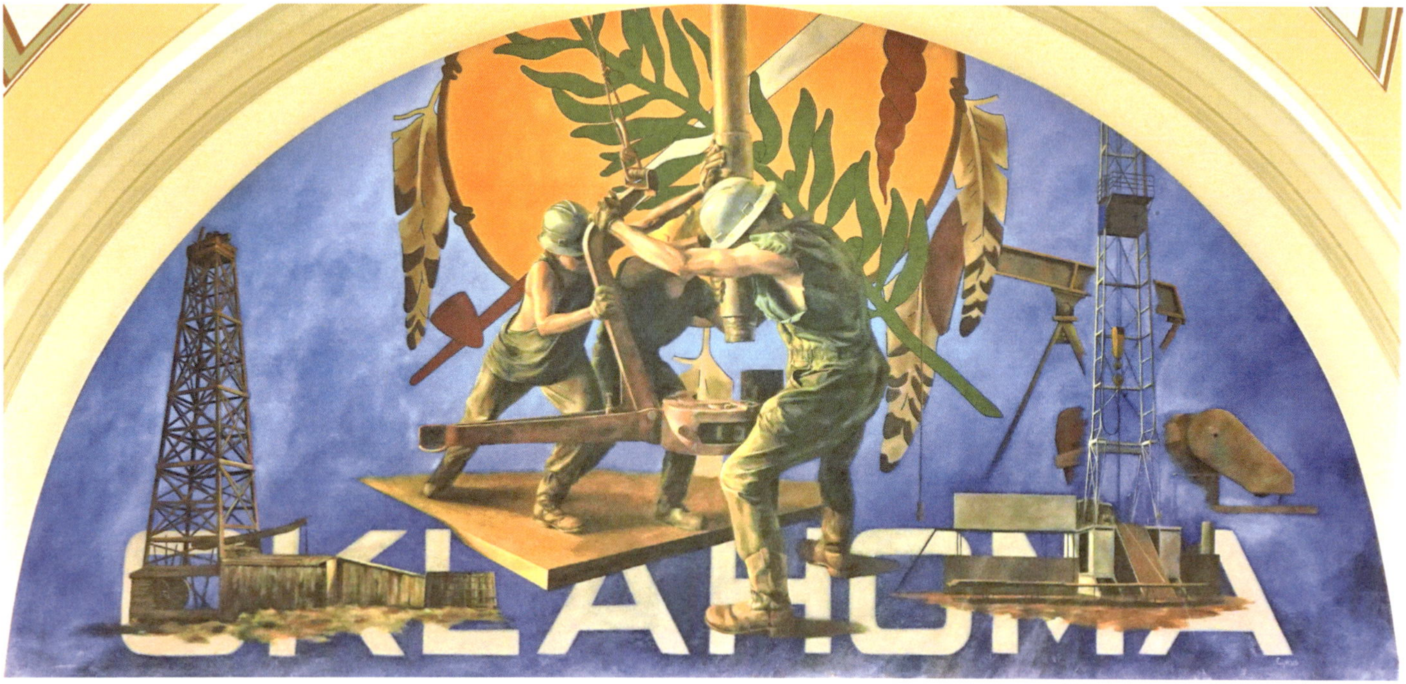

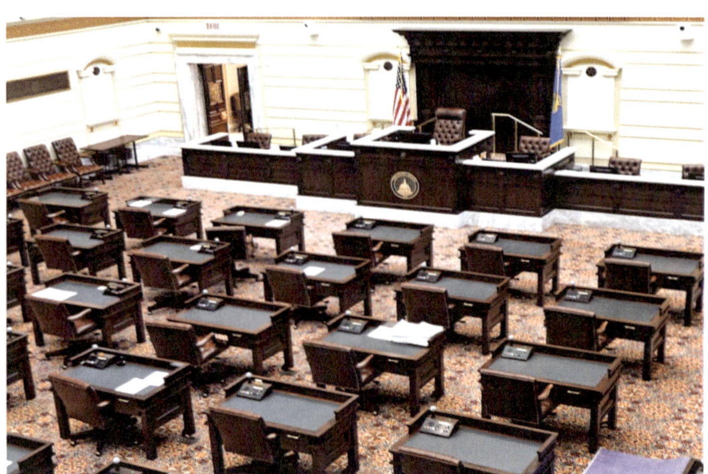

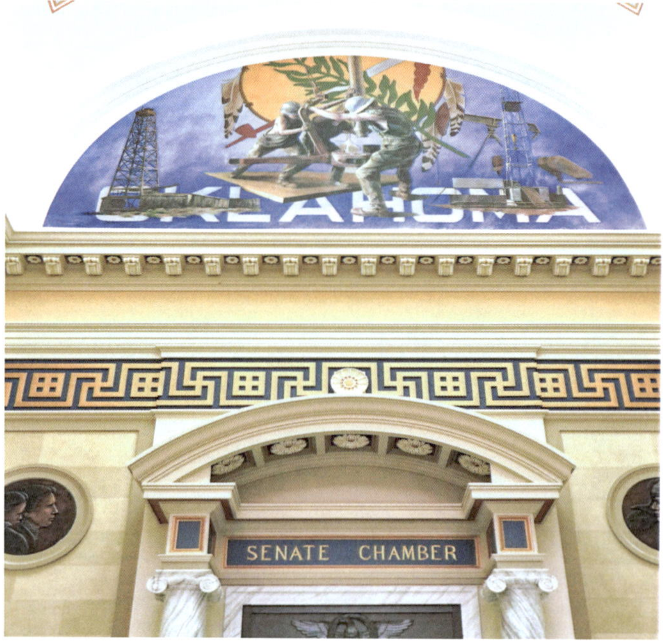

Artist Jeff Dodd's *Oklahoma Black Gold* painting in the lunette above the Senate Chamber door highlights the oil industry in the state. It was commissioned in 1996.

Senate Chamber

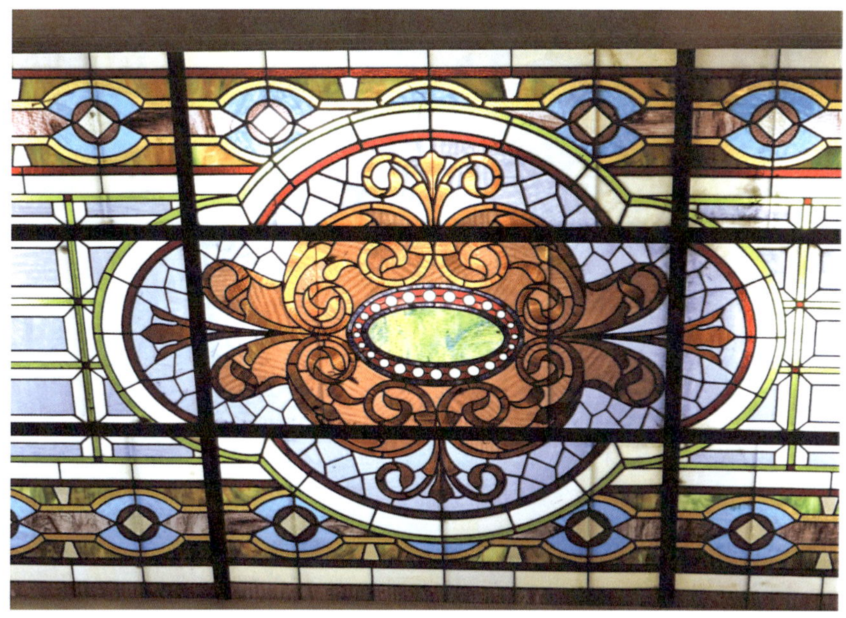

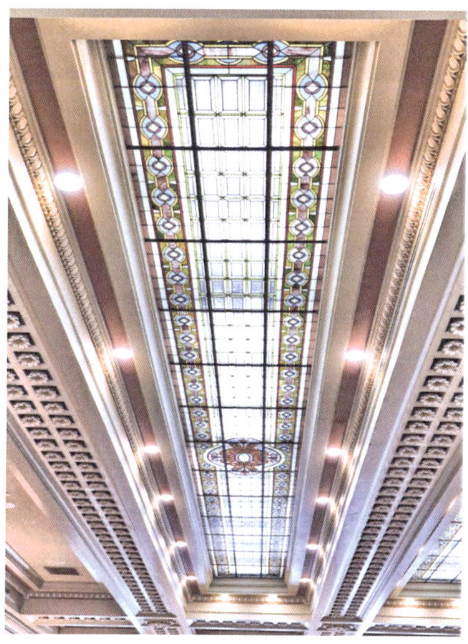

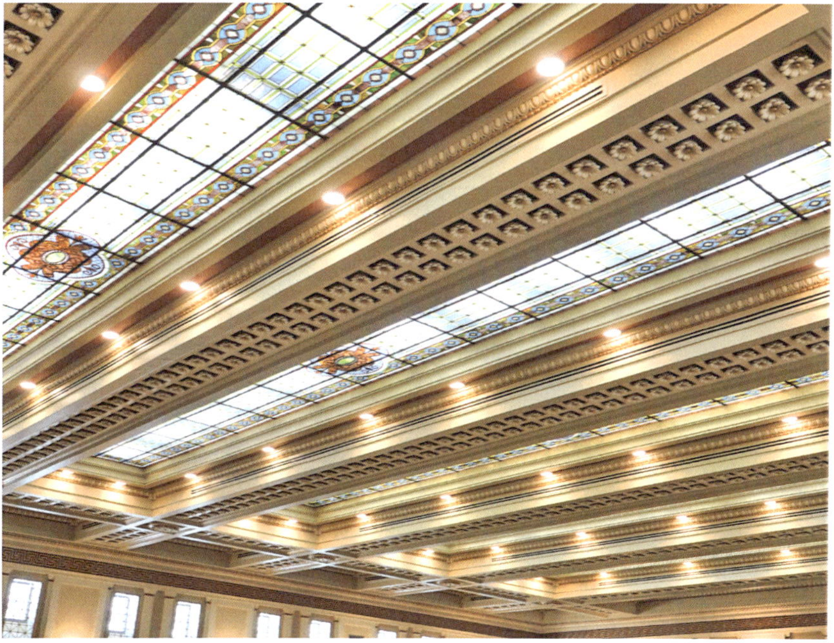

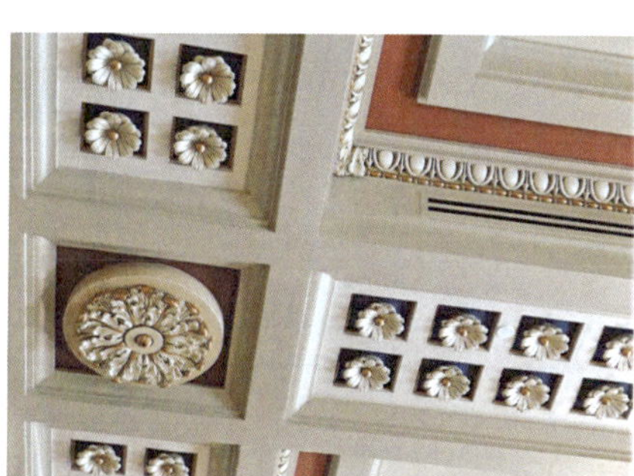

Stained-glass ceilings adorn both the Senate and House of Representatives chambers. The Senate is more decorative than the House panels.

House of Representatives Chamber

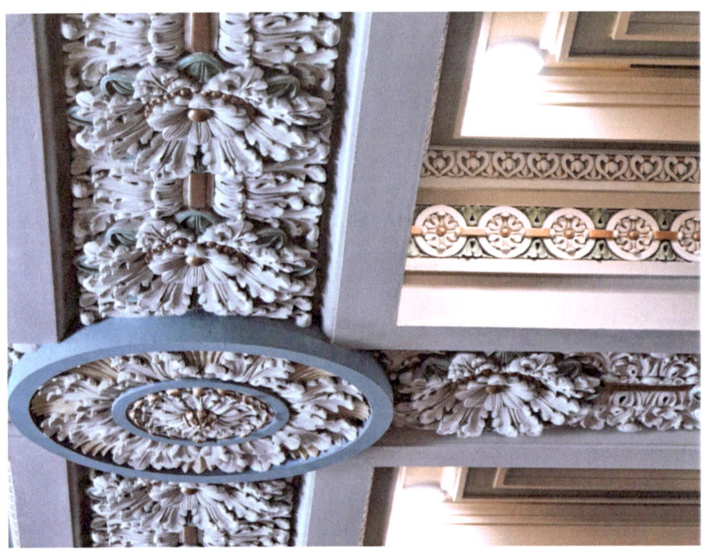

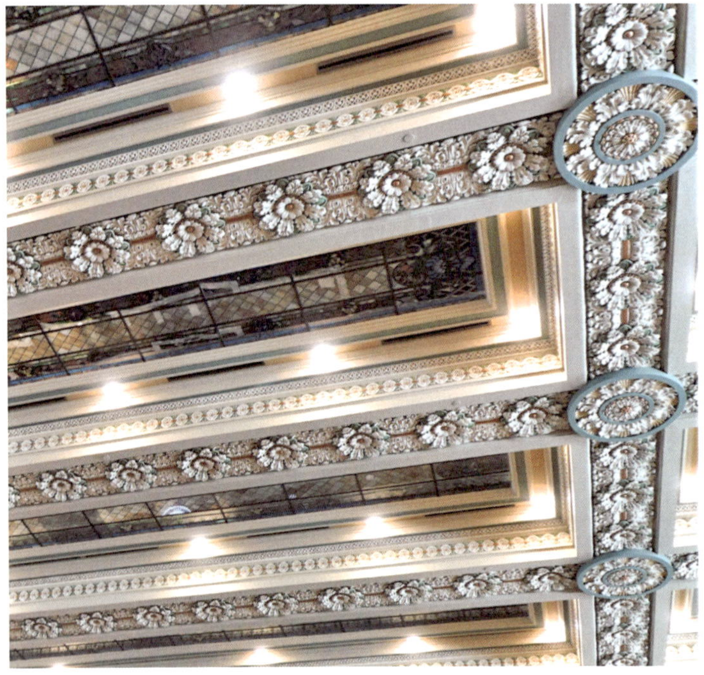

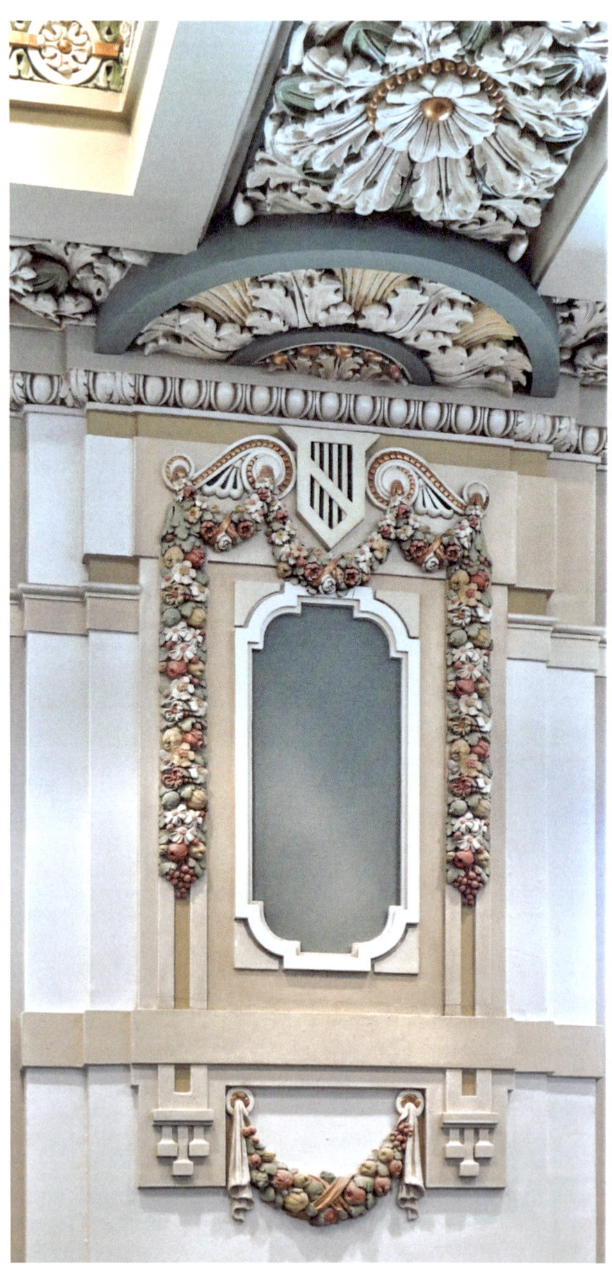

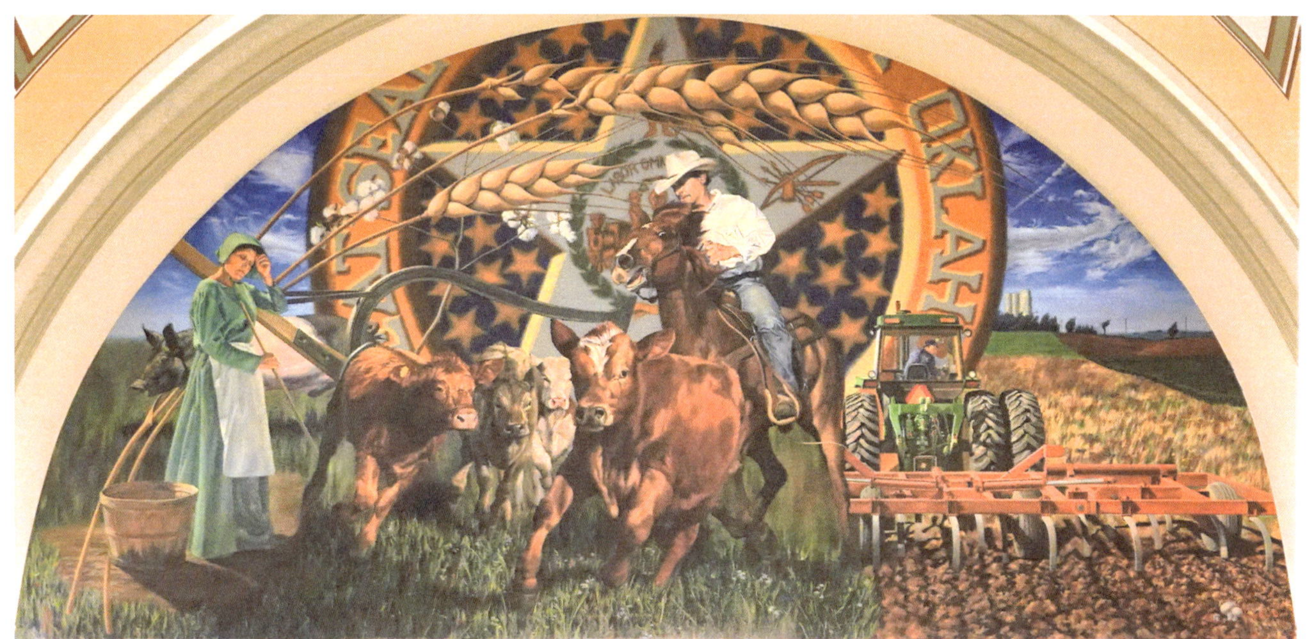

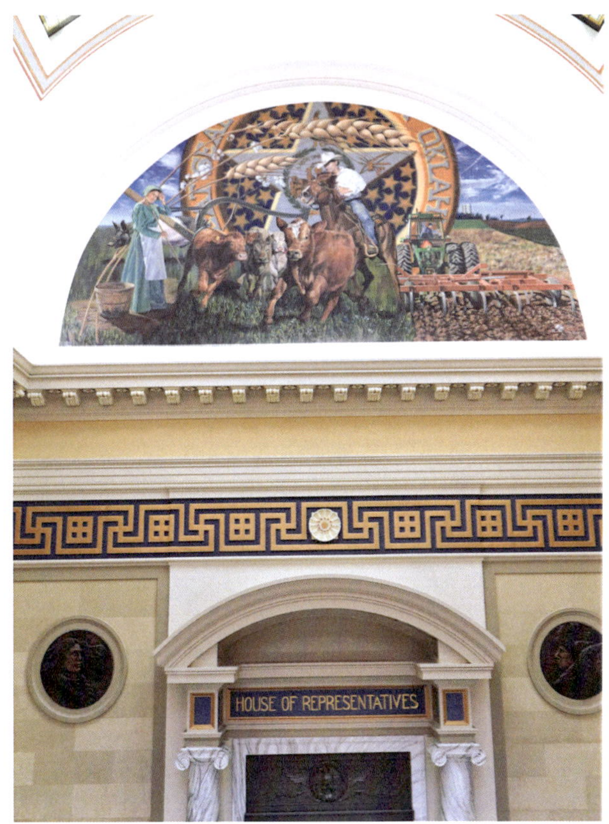

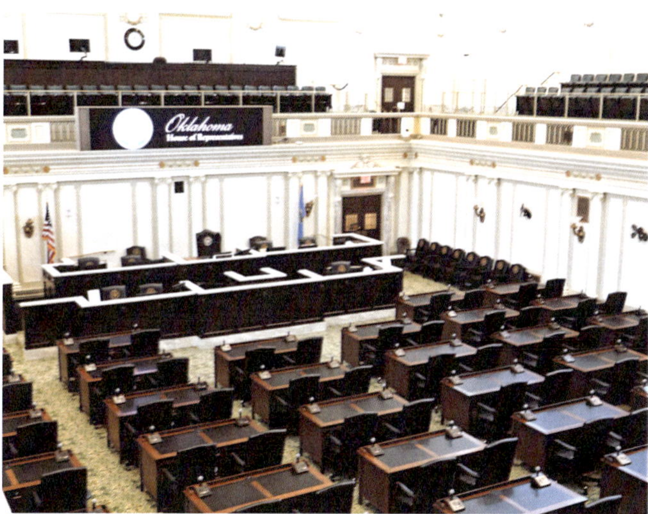

Artist Jeff Dodd's *We Belong to the Land* painting is displayed in the lunette above the House of Representatives Chamber door, highlighting the significant contributions that agriculture has made to the history of the state. Dedicated on Mar. 16, 1999.

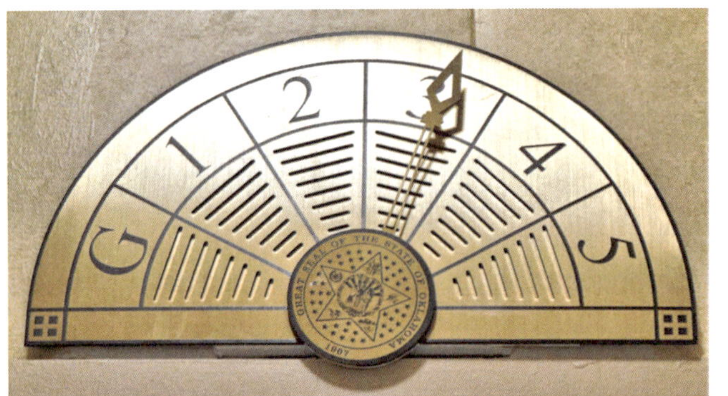

Art Deco

Brass light fixtures throughout the building and the brass elevator doors capture the art deco style when the building was designed in 1914.

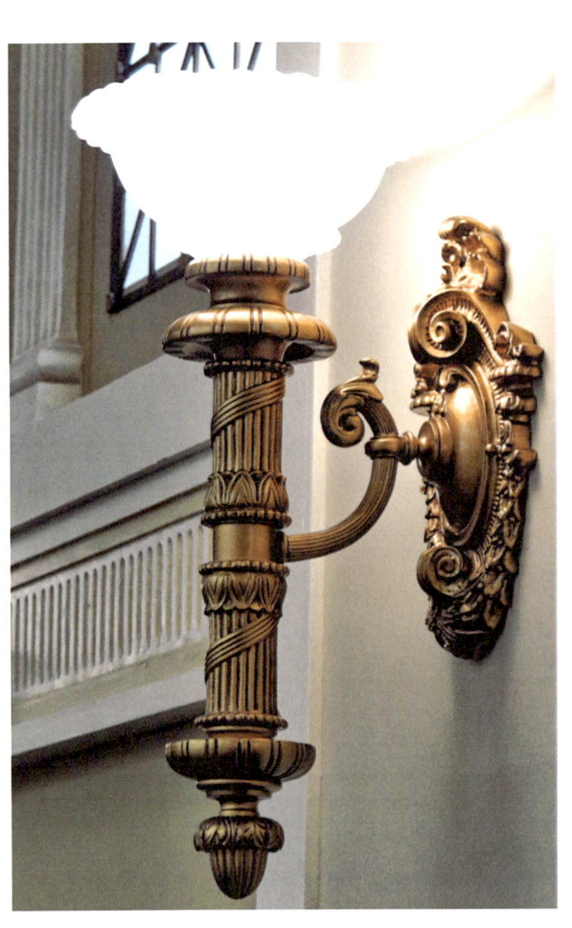

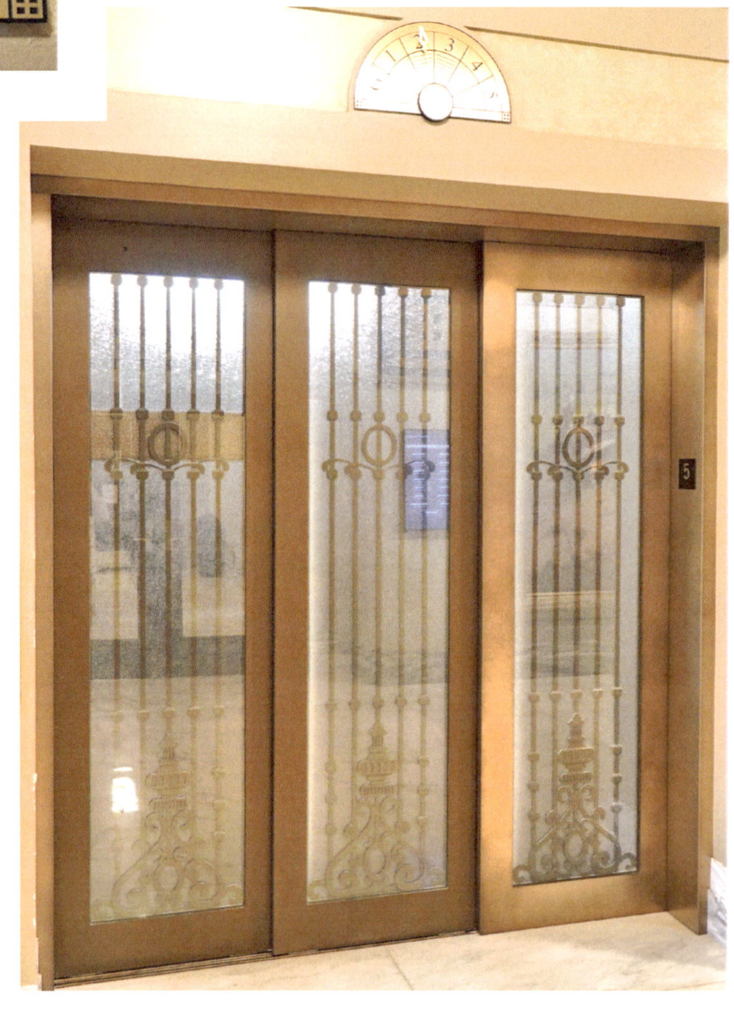

Governor's Office

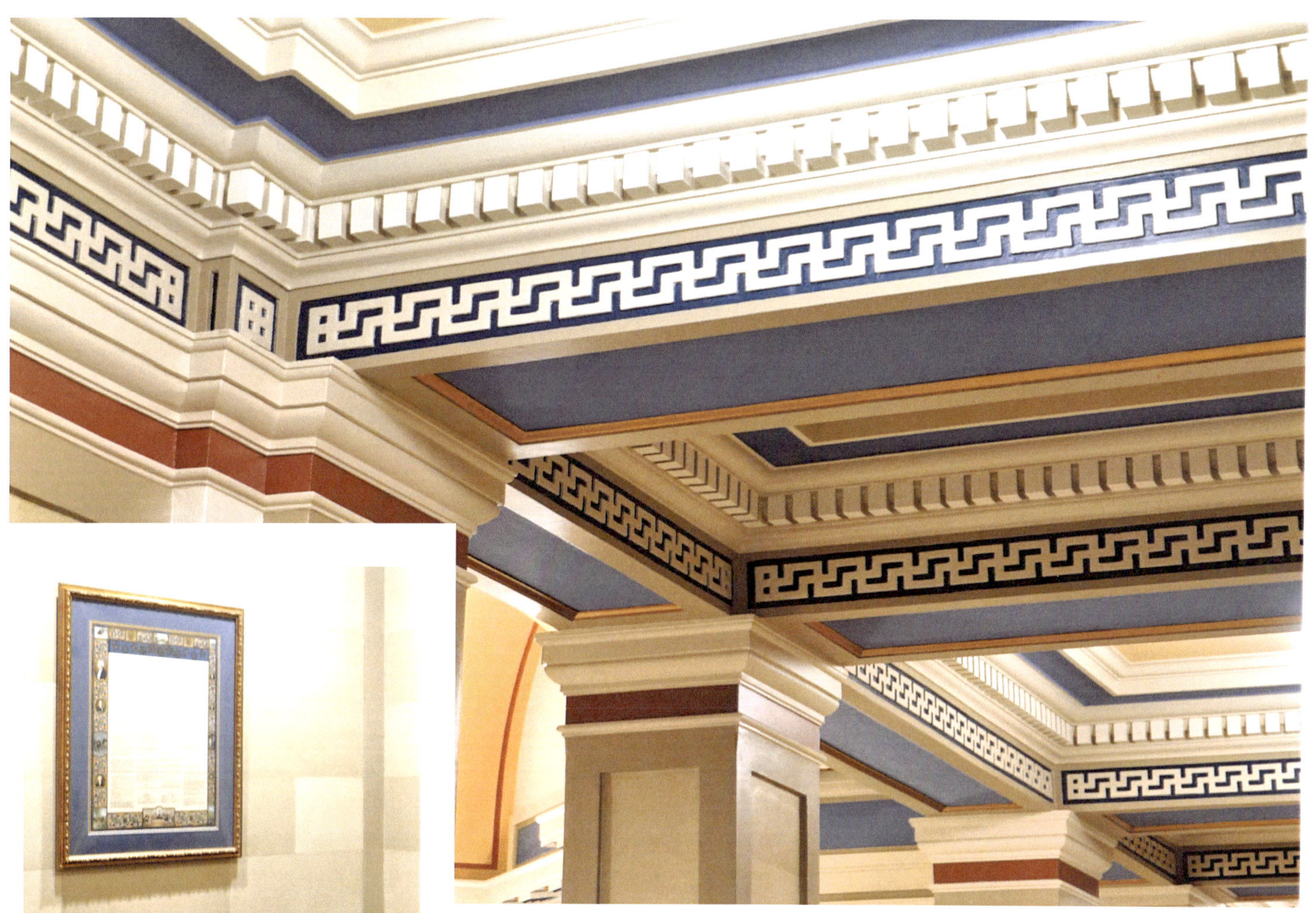

The ceilings in the Governor's office waiting area capture the color scheme of the interior design of the capitol.

Oklahoma State Seal

The Great Seal of Oklahoma was officially adopted in 1907.

The five rays of the star hold the seals of the Five Civilized Tribes — Cherokee (upper left point), Chickasaw (top point), Choctaw (upper right point), Creek (lower left point), and Seminole (lower right point), all of whom have a major presence in the state.

The five-pointed star, surrounded by 45 stars, represents the 45 U.S. states that existed prior to Oklahoma's statehood in 1907. The large star in the middle of the seal represents Oklahoma's admission as the 46th state.

The center of the star contains the territorial seal. It contains the words Labor omnia vincit, meaning "Labor Conquers All Things," above the figures. An olive branch of peace surrounds the territorial seal.

Columbia is the center figure, representing justice and statehood. She is surrounded by an American pioneer on her right and the Native American on her left, both of whom are shaking hands beneath the scales of justice, symbolizing equal justice between the Anglo and Native American races in Oklahoma and on the part of the federal government.

Beneath the trio is the cornucopia of plenty, and behind is the sun of progress and civilization.

The words "Great Seal of the State of Oklahoma" and the date of statehood, 1907, encircle the seal.

The seal appears above the capitol's grand entrance door, on the first floor of the rotunda, and the oculus at the top of the inner dome. It also is the center of the floor indicator above the elevator doors.

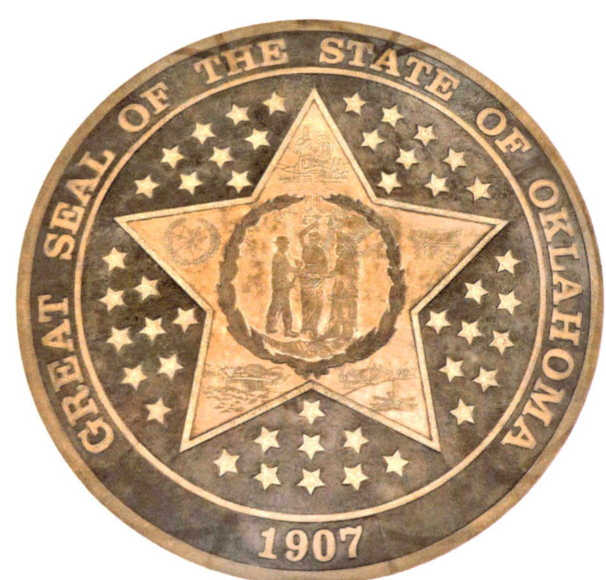

About the Photographer

Jane Moorman describes herself as an adventurer who loves to drive backroads to see what there is to see.

During her 30-year journalism career, Jane honed her photographic skills as a photojournalist, including covering high school sporting events.

A friend once said, "I wish I could see the world as Jane sees it. Finding the beauty in things that most of us don't take time to see."

Upon retiring in 2021, Jane decided there was a lot of her native country she had not visited, including each state's capitol, so she began her journey of exploring the USA.

She currently lives in Albuquerque, New Mexico, but says her real home is on the road.